# GET ME THE RECIPE

vegan recipe ~~blog~~ cookbook

Contains 22 recipes that serve at least 5 people, can be made in one pot and are always under 20 dollars.

(and it has some advice and stuff)

written by Devon Moran

designed by Lauren Boggio & Ali Ándino

# INTRODUCTION

Hello! I am Devon and I am so flattered and happy that you decided to read this book. I have been developing recipes for the last ten years living in different areas of the United States, and for a lot of that time I resided in some small apartments with very little kitchen space. I also spent many years living paycheck to paycheck, but I always made it a huge priority to cook for myself and to make healthy, filling and delicious meals. Through job changes, location changes and life changes, the time I spent cooking remained the most stable in my life. It was my time to express myself, learn and experiment, and I can't imagine not having experienced those thousands of hours of creativity.

After I graduated from college, I wanted to make some healthy changes and enhance my lifestyle. I thought the best way to do that was to take control of what I was eating, so I started cooking. I really didn't know anything at the beginning other than that it felt good to make my own food and that I enjoyed the cooking almost as much as the eating. I also knew right away that I was good at it and that I wanted to continue working and improve.

I realized pretty quickly that listening to my instincts made me feel naturally comfortable in the kitchen. I felt so comfortable that I started creating recipes myself. As the weeks passed, I got more confident and wanted to share what I was making, so I began cooking for my family and then my friends. I grew to love making food for as many people as I could, and in 2012, I worked at a youth hostel making breakfast for the guests, which helped me to learn the ins and outs of cooking for large groups of people. I loved that part of the job; adding to the value of these world travelers' vacation.

I wanted to write this book to help guide people who feel nervous or unsure of where to start when it comes to cooking. I understand feeling limited by space, money or kitchen equipment, but you don't have to. I can personally say that I was still able to cook myself dynamic and healthy meals when I lived in an apartment with no counter space, 1 working burner on my incredibly small stove, and an oven that wouldn't get higher than 200 degrees.

I also had 1 pot, 1 pan, a few utensils and a baking sheet, so I was really limited. I got extra creative and continued to meal plan, meal prep, and cook awesome dishes during that entire time period.

I started making "One Pot" meals (before I knew that they were called that) because I didn't have many options, and I LOVED making them. I tried as many different combinations and foods as I could think of and they kept coming out really well. Besides being spatially challenged I also wasn't making a lot of money. This forced me to get savvy about how to find affordable foods and how to efficiently and effectively make choices that would feed me for the longest time without costing me all of my money.

The reason I am telling you this (and why I wanted to publish this book in the first place) was because I want you to be able to do the same thing! I don't want you to ever feel limited or like you can't make yourself healthy and tasty meals with dignity, regardless of the size of your kitchen or your bank account. I want to share my experiences and help you to understand the tips and tricks to overcome any obstacles you are facing. The recipes are all very manageable and designed to help teach you to expand on them as you become more comfortable.

Anyone can cook, including you. I am so excited that I can't even wait any longer, so here we go!

## 1. HOW TO PRACTICE

Like most skills, the best way to improve at cooking is to practice. Also like with most skills, the best way to practice something is to do it as often as possible, like every day! Cooking is like going to the gym or learning an instrument or doing yoga or literally anything else; sometimes it takes a while to notice any real change or improvement but if you stick with it eventually you will. I consider myself to be a very advanced cook at this point and I don't think there is really a single thing that would intimidate me to make, but I still practice.

Being mindful is one of the most important elements of practicing. I completely understand sometimes after a long day that zoning out, putting on music and making dinner is the best way to reward yourself. I have many of those days myself; in fact, there were years at a time where I did that, and it was great. I know my cooking improved because of the daily repetition, but my progress was much slower than the times I have been deliberately mindful of what I was creating.

I don't want the phrase "being mindful" to scare you or "practice" to make you feel like you are doing a chore or have homework. It should be fun and rewarding and if you feel intimidated, start with one small goal and go from there. In a few pages there are instructions on how to make a Flax seed egg, so you could start with that and work on it until you feel like your flax eggs are perfect. There are also so many One Pot meals in this book, so practicing the timing and temperature gaging while you cook is an excellent skill. Right now, I am practicing making my plain white or brown rice better. Nothing fancy, but an area I want to improve, and I have already seen advancement since I began focusing on it.

Do what works the best for you. Use a timer, take notes, use your five senses (More on that coming up!), come up with mantras* that work for you, or get creative and find your own way to be mindful. I know you can do it!

### *SOME MANTRA SAMPLES:

**"Look, Look, I'm A Sick Cook"**
**"I Am Making Something From Something Else. That's Really Cool"**
**"This Food Is My Energy And I Love It"**
**"I Am So Healthy. I Ate A Vegetable Today. New Body Who Dis?"**

## 2. WHAT YOU LIKE

This seems like a really broad statement, and that is probably because it is. There is no limit to the foods, cooking styles, cooking utensils, time of day, length of time, background music or amount of food that you can enjoy. It is helpful to pay attention to how you are feeling. Use the times you feel at ease, happy, confident, excited or any other positive emotion as a gage for what is working for you. If you feel the best using one day to cook 4 things that last you the whole week and you end up cooking for 8 hours straight, you are like me and that's great! If you like cooking right away after work and then waiting a few hours to eat, amazing! If you like dead quiet or heavy metal music or Real Housewives or opera or just conversation on the phone or in person with a friend or family member or your dog or parrot, that is wonderful! If you love getting up and cooking at 4 am before you leave for the day so it's ready for you when you go home, I love it. If you love cooking a huge amount for the whole week, I want to hear more about it. If you like cooking one meal a day, couldn't love it more. Do you see where I am going with this?

You are the one who knows yourself the best. It may seem over the top or dramatic to tell you that instincts are our superpowers and to use them when you are cooking but listen…this is literally how we get out energy. What you make and what you eat is what is going to power you through the day, so why not do anything you can to make it the best experience possible? Listen to your body and determine what feels good for YOU. Don't feel like you have to follow an exact mold of what

to do and don't feel like you have to stay one way forever! I might wake up tomorrow and have the overwhelming urge to only cook after midnight and you know what, I trust myself, so that's what I would do.

This also applies to food. Unless your doctor has given you instructions to do otherwise, don't eat what you don't like! Make sure that you are getting all of the nutrients you need, and it's good to be adventurous and try new things but If you know you don't like something, guess what…you don't have to eat it. You are the cook! You are in charge! Isn't this what we all wait for from the time we are kids? To get to choose what we have for every meal?! Congrats! You have made it. Enjoy it because a lot of other parts of adulting are hard.

I hate tofu, so I don't eat it. I love lentils, so I eat them about 3 times a week. I will try tofu every once in a while, to see if anything's changed or if there is a particular meal that I might like, but for the most part, I'm going to do what I want to do because I am a grown woman. So do what you want and what makes you feel good! You are a boss! But really, make sure you are getting your nutrients.

## 3. HOW TO BE CONFIDENT

So, I just mentioned that your superpower instincts are simmering under the surface ready and waiting for you to use them to learn about your cooking style. Once you start doing that, confidence is right behind it! YAHOO! Confidence is an incomparable tool to help you. You don't have to always be completely 100% positive that something brand new you are trying will come out perfect, but if you have doubts and uncertainty and you only focus on that, it's going to bring you down. Focus on something in the recipe you are excited about or feel good about. As you complete a meal, notice what went well and use that to feel confident next time. Each little success adds a layer of confidence to your cooking skills, so grab onto it and own it. You have every right to feel good and proud and happy about what you are doing, so go on with your bad self!

## 4. TO KNOW YOU DESERVE HEALTHY AND GOOD FOOD NO MATTER WHAT

I really, really, REALLY want to stress to you that no matter what your circumstances are, including your job, your house, your personal life, your age, your race, what grades you got in high school, what car you drive or if you take the bus **YOU ARE WORTHY OF GOOD AND HEALTHY FOOD THAT IS PREPARED WITH DIGNITY! I CAN'T STRESS THIS ENOUGH.** There are ways to get food and ways to be creative with making it. I am going to let you read the recipes to see how little is actually required to make a delicious and nutritious meal that serves 6-10 people. We can get creative together and make sure that there is nothing to limit you from getting what you need to learn and grow into the best cook you can be.

There are a lot of factors telling us that our status establishes our worth, but I am here to say that in the kitchen, that is complete B.S.- I can't and I shan't with any of that craziness. You are worthy and capable. Having feelings of negativity or that you don't deserve to eat well are more dangerous than any diet. I hope that you aren't feeling like this to begin with, but if you are, let's put a stop to that ASAP, ok?

**YOU ARE AWESOME, IF FOR NO OTHER REASON THAN THAT YOU DECIDED TO BUY MY BOOK, AND YOU SHOULD FEEL AWESOME. YES!**

## 5. YOU DON'T NEED A BUNCH OF FANCY STUFF TO COOK

This ties into the previous bullet point, but I wanted to get a bit more specific. Like in every other area of life, the kitchen industry has a LOT of stuff and a LOT of ways to spend money. I totally understand feeling like you don't know where to start with shopping for your kitchen if you have a small budget, or no budget. I don't know what some of these books or lists that suggest "needed items" or "How to get your dream kitchen" assume we all do for a living, but I have bills to pay. I have worked hard and accumulated a nice collection of supplies after many years, but there were times that dropping a few hundred dollars on bowls and spoons was not an option. I have made a list for you of things that I would consider necessary to regularly cook and feed yourself. You can get creative though. For a while, I didn't have a lid for any of my pots, so I used a cookie sheet. Don't judge me! I made it work and you can too. I am going to take a lot of the guessing out of it for you, so take the time to check out my suggestions in a few pages and get yourself set up, without stressing and wondering if you need a whole load of other things you have no idea how to get or how to afford.

Also, I know that sometimes it can feel like a total lame bummer to be working in a small space. I have absolutely been there and the times that I hated my kitchen never felt good. I don't want to tell you to just look on the bright side and that everything will be rainbows and unicorns, because that is not always the case. I will say to try to reclaim the space and the time you are cooking as your own, whatever that means to you. Try to take some of the power back; maybe thinking "Yah, this sucks and my kitchen is small, but I love this time I get to cook because I put on the Daily Show from last night and I feel like Trevor Noah is my best friend and I laugh and it makes the time seem quicker." You can also make that the time of day you listen to your favorite podcast or something that makes you feel good and takes the suckyness out of it a bit. It can still be fun, I promise.

## 6. USE ALL 5 SENSES

Exactly how it sounds. Look, listen, touch, smell, taste. Look at the food and watch how it changes as it cooks. This seems so simple but one of the ways I first learned that something was done was "Does it look like I want to eat it?". Listen to how the pot sounds. If it is covered and you hear a lot of bubbling, the heat might be too high, so check it and turn it down. You can also listen to hear sizzling and (hopefully not) the fire alarm.

Touch can be relative. You can use a utensil to touch and test the softness of your food or hover your hand above to see how warm it is. Use a fork if you need to. And stir from the bottom. Smell is obvious, you want to see how amazing the flavors are blending together! Also, keep your nose our for burning smells. Really bad and no fun at all.

Finally, taste. *Make sure you added enough garlic salt.*

**Try to see if you can implement this into every recipe you make, even it is in a small way.**

## 7. HOW TO WATCH THE MEAL COOK WITH YOUR EYES AND LET THE FOOD TEACH YOU WHAT TO LOOK FOR

This is just an extension of using your sight like mentioned above, but I wanted to expand on it to say really pay attention and watch what happens. Check out how certain ingredients change shape and form as they cook. Look at how the liquid absorbs or evaporates. Try to get in tune with what the food is doing. These observations will help you to learn. Pay attention to what works and make a note of what to look for next time. You will be an expert before you know it.

## 8. STIRRING FROM THE BOTTOM

I think this is in the directions of every single one of my recipes because it is really important with One pot meals. You want to make sure that the food doesn't stick to the pot or pan, because if it does, it is either burning or it needs more liquid. It is good to get into the habit of checking the temperature of your burner by gaging how the food is cooking, because every stove is different. While you are getting to be an expert on that, make sure you are giving whatever you are making your attention and time and NOT BURNING IT. Stir from the bottom. Trust me.

## 9. TASTE TEST

Again, make sure you used enough garlic powder. And also to see if it's to your liking. Do you need to add anything or use less of something next time? You will master this too, I know it.

## 10. BE SAFE

Use a potholder. If you don't have one and are using a dish towel, fold it over three times and protect your hand. If you don't have a dish towel, use a regular towel, or your ex's t-shirt you have been meaning to throw away. Make sure there is nothing flammable near your stove. Make sure you aren't using a dull knife. Pay attention when you are using the stove. Be careful when handling a hot pot that is heavy. Let the food cool before you taste test or put it anywhere near your body.

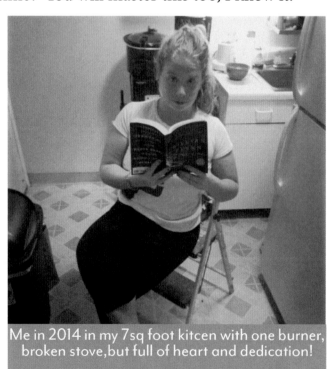

Me in 2014 in my 7sq foot kitcen with one burner, broken stove, but full of heart and dedication!

## 11. WHERE TO FIND STUFF AND HOW TO SAVE MONEY

Alright, here is where you learn all of the really important stuff. I recommend joining any "buying/ selling" Facebook group you can find for your town or neighborhood. Sometimes there are groups where people just straight up give things away. Keep an eye out for kitchen supplies on there and if you see something good, grab it. Also, let people know you are working on building your kitchen. They might keep you in mind if they are getting rid of certain items. I don't think there are many tag sales anymore, but if you see signs for them, check them out.

If you don't have a car, or you are in a position where you are able to buy 1 or 2 small things every paycheck, I think an amazon prime membership is a good investment. You can fill a cart and on pay day, chip away at your list. They have good prices and free shipping and you can get it the next day. You can also get your groceries delivered, which seems like fancy person thing to do but it actually can be really economically smart. You can get a LOT of deals as a prime member, and you won't be distracted by opportunity buys all over the place. Also, a lot of the time you can get a 10% or $10 off coupon from your order. I have not used Instacart, so I don't have much to offer on that, but if you are without a car and would need to take an uber to the store, it may make more sense to have your food delivered. It really does make a difference in controlling the items you get as well.

If you ride your bike as your main source of transportation (I did this for years while living in California), and ride to get your groceries, get a good sturdy basket. You can get a second hand one, or spring for a new one because the sturdier the better. You want to make sure that the basket is deep so you can easily fit your bags without spilling them. Also, get a backpack; I highly recommend the Under-armor Brand because they have a LOT of room, they are strong, and they are sweat proof and waterproof. Plus, they have a lot of pockets so you can keep your keys and wallet separate so they won't get buried at the bottom of your bag. It's annoying when you go to pay, and you can't find what you are need or when you get home and can't find your keys because they are under all the food! Pack your groceries into the backpack with the heaviest items on the bottom. This not only helps your food not get crushed, but it will help you keep your balance while riding. Also, get a helmet. I didn't have a grocery store within 3 miles of my apartment for several months, and this was before uber so I was biking everywhere. DO NOT hang your bags from the handlebars, especially if they are plastic. The spokes from your wheel will tear them apart and you will have your stuff all over the road.

Check out farmers' markets. I know they have a reputation of being expensive, but they have the best quality of vegetables and if you are a meal planner and are able to make a list of exactly what you need and budget it out, you can get good values and good food within your means. You can also become friendly with the vendors and they can keep you posted on what they will have week

# WHAT I WANT TO TEACH YOU

to week, and sometimes you can offer to buy any slightly less than perfect produce for a discounted price. Not every vendor will be into this, but a lot are and actually appreciate you taking the food.

Eat what's in season. There are a lot of studies that say that we are supposed to get back to basics and do this anyway, but it's a good way to help your budget. Whatever is in season will be cheapest, so stick to meals that involve root veggies in the winter, greens in the summer, etc.

Cook with Vegetable broth. It is cheaper than olive oil, and way healthier. It is a really nice way to sauté vegetables or make rice, quinoa, barley, or any other starch base. I will explain more in the recipes.

Shop at The Grocery Outlet. I wish they had these all over the country and hopefully they will one day, but if you live close enough to one hit that place up as often as you can! The deals are incredible.

Shop at Trader Joe's. I hope you are lucky enough to live near one and if you do, they have really good prices on frozen vegetables and fruits, and dried foods. They also have unique sauces and mixes, so grab a few of those and try them out as an add on to your recipes. This will help you become more confident and dynamic with your cooking. You can also ask for a gift card for any holiday or your birthday.

Meal Plan. I know it's not the most exciting and sometimes it can feel like a bummer to decide what you are going to eat a week in

advance, but it helps. If you know exactly what you need, you can budget before you go shopping and spend accordingly. You will also have exactly what you need and not end up with a bad of spoiled spring mix in your drawer a week later.

Check out food banks. A lot of time's there is really high-quality food donated, and Trader Joe's donates any food that is dented or slightly below excellent quality every single day, so the places that they work with can get up to thousands of dollars of quality food every day. Go check it out!

This might sound weird, but just be nice and open to people in general. Be friendly and kind and sometimes things will come up that a friend or co-worker no longer needs, and they are happy to pass it along to you. I also really believe in the power of asking the universe for what you want. I have had many, many times in my life that I have directly said "I want 'x'" and within a few days gotten it either on sale at a store or from a neighbor giving it away. Try it out; what do you have to lose? Then,when you find yourself in a position where you are ready to give something away or help someone else, do it!

Also, none of the products or places I listed sponsor me in any way, this is truly based on years of experience of figuring out what worked for me.

## 12. Watching and Learning Temperature

Every single stove and oven I have had has been a little bit different, so you need to get to know what you are working with.  It is also good to pay attention and practice the different time and temperature it takes for different items to cook the way you like it.  If you like your lentils a little crunchy, make you cook them for less time.  Same thing with vegetables.  You can take control of this and you can totally master it, the main thing to do is pay attention.  Make a note.  Remember for next time.

## 13. Have Fun!

No long crazy story for this one.  Fun is what it's all about. And be proud of yourself for taking this on and taking control of your diet.  I am really proud of you!

# ESSENTIAL THINGS YOU NEED RELIABLY COOK FOR YOURSELF

## POT

You need a steady, reliable, big pot for most of these meals. It's worth it. Get one from amazon or a thrift store. Try to get a lid too because you need to cover the pot for most of these recipes AND if you get one you don't need to get a strainer. You can use the lid to strain the water one.

## SAUCEPAN

A cute little pot with a handle. They are helpful. Not completely dire if you have a pot and a frying pan, but they can make life easier.

## POTHOLDER OR TOWEL OR EX'S TSHIRT-DUH.

Don't burn yourself

## BAKING SHEET

It's good for roasting vegetables and can work as a lid for a pot in a pinch (I've been there)

## SPATULA

Needed to stir and sauté your vegetables in the frying pan.

## WOODEN SPOON

Gotta stir that food! And Stir from the bottom! These are like $2, so grab one. It's worth it.

## FRYING PAN

If you can get a small one and a big one, nice! If not, just get a big one. It will cover all of your needs

## TUPPERWARE

For my meal prepping homies. You need a place to store those meals! Be cautious about lending it out (make sure you can trust the people you give it to return it!) and it doesn't all have to match. If you get Chinese food or Indian food or any other take out that give you those reusable plastic containers hold onto those badboys for sure!

## A SHARP KNIFE

this is worth it to spend a bit more money on. It doesn't have to be $100, but maybe $10-15. You want to be safe and if you have a dull knife you will end up frustrated.

## 1/3 MEASURING CUP & 1/2 MEASURING CUP

if you can get all of them, awesome, but if you have these two you can measure out anything else you need.

## 1 TSP AND A TBSP

You don't need the others; you can do the math needed to get any other measurements

## CUTTING BOARD

Don't not get your deposit back because you destroyed your counter.

## CAN OPENER

I have a lot of canned beans in these recipes. Get a medium good one, not the cheapest. It sucks when you buy it and it stops working and you have to buy another after you only used it twice.

# INGREDIENTS TO HAVE AROUND THE KITCHEN AT ALL TIMES:

**SALT**
**OLIVE OIL**
(I use vegetable broth a lot because olive oil is expensive, but you can get a big and good bottle from Trader Joe's and use it sparingly.)
**GARLIC POWDER**
**PEPPER**
**SMOKED PAPRIKA**
**TURMERIC**
**CURRY POWDER**
**GRAHAM MASALA**

**LENTILS**
**FLOUR**
(good for sauces and god forbid a grease fire)
**RICE**
**BEANS**
**GROUND FLAX**
**VEGETABLE BROTH**
**CANNED BEANS**
(cheap and a great thing to eat on their own if needed)

*I listed these because they are my favorite spices. There are about 46 million in the spice aisle and it can be really overwhelming so these are good to start with. If there is something you know you like, get that too! They are about $2 each and you only need to replace them every few months.*

# BASIC AND HELPFUL "HOW TO" TIPS:

## 1. HOW TO COOK BEANS:

1. If you are working with dried beans, they need to soak for 24 hours. Leave them in a bowl or a pot overnight.

2. When you are ready to cook them, put them in the pot with 2 cups of vegetable broth for every 1 cup of beans. Add salt, pepper, garlic powder and smoked paprika to the pot and heat on high.

3. Bring the broth to a boil, and then cover the pot and reduce the heat to low. You want there to be a slight simmer. They need to cook for about 2 hours but check on them often and stir from the bottom.

## 2. HOW TO CARAMELIZE AN ONION:

1. Make sure you have an onion, and 2/3 cup olive oil OR vegetable broth.

2. Slice the onion down the middle, and then cut longways into 1/4 inch pieces.

3. Heat the liquid in a frying pan on med/high. Add the onion and coat completely. Let it sauté, stirring consistently for 6-8 minutes. The onions should be soft and translucent, and have a texture similar to caramel, which make sense based on the name!

## 3. HOW TO BOIL BEETS:

1. Wash your beets well. I like the skin on, but some people don't so peel them if you are one of those.

2. Put in a small sauce pan and cover them with water.

3. Bring to a boil, and let it go for 30 minutes. Remove and strain, and wait until the are cool enough to slice up and eat.

## 4. HOW TO MASSAGE KALE:

1. Have Kale, Olive Oil and White Vinegar ready to go.

2. Wash the Kale, put it in a bowl, add 1/2 cup of olive oil and 2 Tbsp of vinegar.

3. Wash your hands, and get right in there and start literally massaging it. It will take 2-3 minutes, and the kale will release moisture and become soft.

# BASIC AND HELPFUL "HOW TO" TIPS:

## 5. HOW TO BAKE A POTATO OR A SWEET POTATO

1. Preheat the oven to 375.

2. Get your russet potato and some olive oil

3. Poke 8-12 holes in the potato with a fork.

4. Drizzle the potato with olive oil

5. Place potato on a baking sheet or right on the rack.

6. Bake for 50 minutes

## 6. HOW TO STEAM BROCCOLI:

1. Make sure you have a sauce pan and a steaming basket.

2. Put about 1 inch of water in the pan, make sure it doesn't go over the top of the basket.

3. If you bought a head of broccoli, not florets, cut it up into florets.

4. Bring the inch of water to a boil, put the basket in the pot and cover.

5. If you aren't trying to be super healthy and are looking to indulge, ad a tbsp of butter to the pot. Let the broccoli cook for 6 minutes

## 7. HOW TO BAKE SPAGHETTI SQUASH:

1. CAREFULLY cut the spaghetti squash. I am still really bad at this, so I don't have any great advice but use a sharp knife, cut away from you and cut right down the middle.

2. Preheat the oven to 375 degrees.

3. Pull all the seeds and guts out.

4. Drizzle the inside with olive oil. If you have a brush, use that to spread the oil around. Otherwise, use a spoon, or tilt the squash bowl back and forth to spread it.

5. Sprinkle with salt and pepper.

6. Bake for 45-50 minutes.

## 8. HOW TO MAKE A FLAX EGG

1. Get ground flax meal

2. Add 1 tbsp of flax meal to a small bowl

3. Add 2 Tbsp of water and mix it together.

4. Let it sit for 15 minutes. This is equal to 1 egg,
so double or triple the recipe as needed.

# BARLEY, POTATO AND TOMATO SOUP

## INGREDIENTS

**6** Cups of vegetable broth
**1** Cup of ready to cook barley
(Make sure it says ready to cook, otherwise it will take a LONG time to cook)
**3** Large potatoes, chopped into ½ inch pieces
**1** Onion, diced
**2** Cloves of garlic, minced
**1** Tsp salt
**½** Tsp cumin
**1** Tsp paprika
**½** Tsp pepper

**SERVING SIZE** : 8 PORTIONS

**TOTAL TIME**: 1 HOUR AND 15 MINUTES

**COST**: LESS THAN $18

## NUTRITIONAL INFO
**Calories:** 118 • **Protein:** 3g • **Carbs:** 23g
**Fat:** <1g • **Fiber:** 3g • **Sugar:** 3g

## DIRECTIONS

I have always liked the flavor of tomato soup so much, especially when you pair it with a delicious vegan grilled cheese. The only issue I have with it is that I wish there was more to it; I think most of the time the most efficient (meaning they are easy to make and have a lot of nutritional value/fill you up) meals are the best meals. I created this soup to be a robust take on traditional tomato soup, and it helps that it is really easy to make!

In a large pot, bring 4 cups of broth, barley, onion, potatoes, garlic and spices to a boil. Add the can of tomatoes, and reduce heat to low, covering. Every 15 minutes add ½ cup of vegetable broth and stir, repeating this for a total of an hour. The barley and potatoes will be soft and completely immersed in all of the flavors. So simple, but so good. When you taste it, notice each separate flavor and also how they blend together. Notice the texture of the barley and the potatoes and as always, take notes on what you like and what you want to work on, if anything.

Serve this bad boy warm with a vegan grilled cheese, sit there, enjoy, and be glad that there is such a delicious thing in the world for you to eat. **I am so proud of you!**

# COUSCOUS ANTIPASTO

## INGREDIENTS

**1** Cup of couscous
**1** 12 Ounce can of artichoke hearts, drained and chopped into really small pieces
**1** 12 Ounce can of black olives, sliced and chopped
**1** Cup of roasted red peppers, chopped into small pieces
**1** 12 Ounce can of green olives, sliced and chopping
**1** Cup of vegetable broth
**2** Tsp olive oil
**1** Tsp salt
**1** Tsp garlic powder
**½** Cup of capers

**SERVING SIZE :** 5 PORTIONS

**TOTAL TIME**: 35 MINUTES

**COST**: LESS THAN $16

### NUTRITIONAL INFO
**Calories:** 312 • **Protein:** 8g • **Carbs:** 35g
**Fat:** 13g • **Fiber:** 10g • **Sugar:** 2g

## DIRECTIONS

This is a really easy one that is great for when you are feeling a little fancy. It is also a great side/appetizer type dish to bring to a party or potluck and impress everyone there. I love it!

To make the couscous, put the broth, couscous and 1 tsp of olive oil in a small pot and bring the heat to high so that it boils. Once it gets there, remove it from the heat and leave covered for 5 minutes. Fluff it with a fork when it is done, and then add all of the rest of the ingredients either right in the pot or in a bowl, mix it all together and there you go! You so fancy! I hope this helps curb any antipasto craving you have in an easy and affordable way, and I hope you love the dish and that all of your friends do too! **I am so proud of you!**

# BUFFALO CAULIFLOWER SOUP

## INGREDIENTS

**2** Pounds of cauliflower florets, chopped into small pieces
**⅔** Cups of flour
**3** Stalks of celery, chopped into ½ inch pieces
**6** Stalks of asparagus, chopped
**⅓** Cup of red hot sauce or seasoning powder
**⅓** Cup of onion, diced
**5** Cups of vegetable broth
**3** Cloves of minced garlic
**2** Tbsp Italian seasoning

**SERVING SIZE :** 8 PORTIONS

**TOTAL TIME**: 45 MINUTES

**COST**: LESS THAN $18

## NUTRITIONAL INFO
**Calories:** 66 • **Protein:** 3g • **Carbs:** 10g
**Fat:** 0g • **Fiber:** 3g • **Sugar:** 3g

## DIRECTIONS

This is such a cute and fun little take on buffalo wings! I came up with this idea after randomly finding the Frank's Red-Hot seasoning in the grocery store and I bought it so I could work on a recipe for buffalo Cauliflower wings. A couple days later I wanted to make a soup, and still had the cauliflower I bought along with some celery, and I thought that buffalo soup would be an amazing idea. And it's one pot which you know your girl loves!

Add everything except the flour to a large pot and allow the broth to come to a boil. Stir in the flour and allow it to thicken. Reduce the heat and let the soup simmer for 25 minutes, checking and stirring every 6-7 minutes in between. This is a good chance to practice learning about the different textures of soup and to make some notes on how the broth looks different because of the flour. Did you like it more or less than just plain broth? Was it salty and spicy enough for you? If you feel like it, add one or two ingredients to make it your own.

**Serve with some toast and enjoy!**

# DIRECTIONS

I started making this as an option when I was really ballin' on a budget and wanted some good old fashion comfort food that would fill me up and feed me for weeks. I thought you might like it and I wanted to share it with you.  My advice is to go for the dried beans, because as they cook, they really absorb all of the flavor, but you do need to let them soak in water overnight.

Once they have soaked, get out your trusted big pot, and just put everything in there.  Start with 4 cups of the vegetable broth, turn the heat to high and bring it to a boil. Once it is moving and grooving, reduce the heat to low and cover.  It is going to take a while for everything to get fully cooked, so settle in and relax while it is going.  Just make sure the heat isn't too high and check on it every 15 minutes or so, stirring to make sure that nothing is sticking to the bottom of the pot;  adding ½ cup of broth each time you check.  After about an hour, give it a taste and

# RICE AND BEANS

## INGREDIENTS

**1 ½** Cup Of Rice
**1** Cup Of Dried Black Beans
(They Need To Soak Overnight)
Or 2 12 Ounce Cans Of Black
Beans
**6** Cups Of Vegetable Broth
**1** Tsp Salt (More To Taste)
**1** Tsp Garlic Powder (More To
Taste)
**¾** Cups Of Yellow Onion, Diced
**½** Tsp Paprika
**1** Green Pepper, Diced
**1** Tomato, Diced

**SERVING SIZE :** 8 - 10 PORTIONS

**TOTAL TIME**: 3 HOURS

**COST**: LESS THAN $8

## NUTRITIONAL INFO
**Calories:** 170 • **Protein:** 7g • **Carbs:** 28g
**Fat:** 1g • **Fiber:** 6g • **Sugar:** <1g

see how you feel about the seasoning. If you think it needs more of something, add a little bit. Keep it going for another 30 minutes, continuing to check and stir. Patience and love and attention is the secret ingredient in this dish. It sounds cheesy, but it's true. Don't rush through the cooking and pay attention to the way the rice and beans are softening uses all of your senses. Look at them and see if they are softening, listen to the sound it makes as it cooks (it should be a slow and steady simmer), use your sense of smell, use your taste to see how the seasoning is and to see whether the rice and beans are soft enough, and don't touch it while it is too hot, but use your spoon to feel the texture.

This meal is so cozy and wonderful and delicious and filling, and I think it can become a really good staple for you in your meal prep and planning. When you make it for yourself, add something of your own to it and please let me know what it is! **I am so proud of you!**

# JACKFRUIT STIRFRY

## INGREDIENTS

½ Cup of sweet onion, diced
Either **8** small sweet peppers, chopped or
1 green and 1 red pepper, chopped
**5** Stalks of asparagus, chopped into ½
inch pieces
**1** 20 Ounce can of jackfruit in brine,
drained & with the pieces chopped into
small chunks, & the pieces pulled apart
**1 ⅓** Cup of mushrooms, sliced and then
chopped into small pieces
⅔ Cup vegetable broth for the stir fry
¾ Cup of teriyaki sauce
**1** Tsp salt
**1** Tsp garlic powder
½ Tsp all spice
**1 ½** Cup of dried rice if you are making it
**5** Cups of vegetable broth (if you are
making the rice.)
If you are using minute rice or frozen rice,
enough for **1 cup**
**1** Tbsp earth balance if you are making
the rice

**SERVING SIZE :** 6-8 PORTIONS

**TOTAL TIME**: 30 MINUTES

**COST**: LESS THAN $18

## NUTRITIONAL INFO
**Calories:** 188 • **Protein:** 5g • **Carbs:** 39g
**Fat:** 0g • **Fiber:** 3g • **Sugar:** 27g

## DIRECTIONS

I want to start out by saying that making
plain rice is one of my weaknesses. I know
my strengths, and this isn't one of them. I am
much better when it is a rice dish with beans
and lots of vegetables and spices, but I have
never felt like I really mastered making just
plain old rice so there is NO shame in making
minute rice or using the frozen rice from
Trader Joe's (This is my favorite way to make
it). If you want to make the rice from scratch
because that is all you have, I will talk you

through it but don't feel bad if you don't! Get
the job done however it works best for you.

So, here we go:

For the stir-fry, prepare all of the vegetables
and the jackfruit by chopping them so they are
ready to cook. In your largest frying pan, add
the vegetable broth, teriyaki sauce and spices.
Turn the heat to medium and add all of the
vegetables and the jackfruit. From here, you

want to just keep an eye on the mixture and make sure you are stirring it every few minutes so that everything gets heated evenly and is able to cook in the broth. You also want to make sure that the sauce is spread evenly. This is a great thing to practice in your cooking in general, being observant of the way the food is cooking and making sure that nothing gets stuck to the bottom of the pan.

You want to sauté the vegetables until they are visibly much softer. It will take 12-14 minutes. When it is cooked, try a small piece and see how it tastes and add anything else you think will make it taste good. Serve it over the rice and I hope you are proud of yourself! This has been a staple in my diet for years and I made it all the time when I was in my smallest kitchen ever.

If you are making the rice, you will need a small saucepan. Give it a quick coating of cooking spray and get the vegetable broth ready. It's not that there are a lot of steps, it is just important to get the right consistency because life is too short to eat undercooked rice! So, I am the vegetable broth queen and I use that instead of water for everything. It has more sodium BUT it also adds a lot of flavor and I find you need to add way less salt.

Bring 3 cups of broth or water, 1 tsp salt and the earth balance to a boil in the small saucepan. Once it is boiling, add the rice. Reduce the heat so the rice is simmering, and cover. It will need to cook like this for 15-20 minutes, and you should check on it every few minutes and stir it from the bottom to make sure nothing is sticking to the bottom of the pot. This was the biggest struggle I had for years with rice, so it's a good habit to just check on it and really make sure the heat is not on too high. You also don't want it to be on too low, or else it will cook really slowly.

When all of the liquid has been absorbed and the rice is soft, fluff it with a fork. Serve it in a bowl with the stir fry on top. Making rice is a good skill to take notes on and to practice, because rice is just so wonderful. Or you can make sure you have a decent supply of the frozen rice on hand. Both are great, just like you!

# BLACK BEAN ARTICHOKE & HASHBROWN PATTIES

## INGREDIENTS

**8** Red potatoes
**1** 12 ounce can of black beans, drained
**1** 12 ounce can of artichoke hearts, drained
**¼** cup of hoisin sauce
**2** "Eggs" worth of egg replacer
**2** Tbsp cornstarch
**1** Tsp salt
**1** Tsp garlic powder
**⅓** Cup olive oil

**SERVING SIZE :** 10 POR-TIONS

**TOTAL TIME**: 40 MINUTES

**COST**: LESS THAN $16

## NUTRITIONAL INFO
**Calories:** 188 • **Protein:** 8g • **Carbs:** 41g
**Fat:** <1g • **Fiber:** 10g • **Sugar:** 5g

## DIRECTIONS

This is a fun, healthy recipe I made by accident when I was trying to make veggie burgers for the first time. I wanted to use black beans because they are cheap and filling and have so much nutritional value, and all of my favorite Frozen Veggie Burgers have potatoes in them, so I wanted to use those as the two staple ingredients.

I was intimated to make veggie burgers and I didn't know how they would turn out because I have never made them before. To be honest, these turned out way more like potato pancake/fritters than burgers, so I decided to stick with that.
This is probably the most challenging recipe in the book, but it is still totally manageable, and I KNOW you can do it.

Put the potatoes in a large pot, cover them with water and heat on high, bringing it to a boil. Let it boil for 20 minutes, then drain the potatoes into a strainer and let stand.

Make the egg replacer eggs (follow instructions for Red Mill) for flax eggs use 1 ½ tbsp water for 1 tbsp ground flax seed, and let it stand for 15 minutes.

In a large bowl, mush the beans with a fork. Add the potatoes and mush those as well, making a similar consistency to a mashed potato. Add all the over ingredients and mix well. Get it really all blended together. Then, form the mixture into patties using your hands.

Heat the olive oil in a frying pan over medium/high heat and carefully add the patties. Cook on each side for 5 minutes, until each side is crispy.

So many groovy options for serving this one! It works as a breakfast with ketchup and hot sauce, as a snack after the gym, or on a bun with onions and tomatoes. Let me know how you enjoyed it! Was there anything you added to make it more your style? Email me and let me know; **I am so proud of you!**

# MEDITERRANEAN QUINOA
# WITH CHICKPEAS

## INGREDIENTS

**1** Cup of quinoa
**2** Cups of vegetable broth
**½** Cup of chopped olives
**½** Cup of diced sundried tomatoes
**¾** Cup of chickpeas
**¼** Chopped fresh parsley
**½** Cup of diced cucumber
**¼** Cup of olive oil
**1** Tbsp lemon juice
**2** Minced cloves of garlic
**1** Tsp salt
**1** Tsp pepper

**SERVING SIZE :** 6 PORTIONS

**TOTAL TIME**: 30 MINUTES

**COST**: LESS THAN $15

## DIRECTIONS

As I developed as a cook, I taught myself how to use different flavors and ingredients to embody different cuisines. I like to use coconut, tomato paste, graham marsala, curry powder and turmeric for a "Thai" style dish, lots of curry and tomatoes for "Indian", roasted red peppers, olives and capers for "antipasto or Italian", paprika, chili powder, garlic and peppers for "Mexican" and sundried tomatoes, cucumbers, olives and red onions for a sort of Mediterranean Dish. This is one of those, and it is easy, tasty and a cool unique take on an appetizer or salad for a party. So let's get going so you can be the most popular person in the room! It's also great for meal prep and to have for lunch through the week.

### NUTRITIONAL INFO
**Calories:** 237 • **Protein:** 6g • **Carbs:** 21g
**Fat:** 13g • **Fiber:** 4g • **Sugar:** 4g

Start by cooking the quinoa according to the package but sub the vegetable broth for the water. When it is done and fluffy, add to a large bowl. Add the rest of the ingredients, stir, and that's literally it. You're done. I told you it was easy! Now enjoy!

What did you like? What would you change? Was anything confusing? Did you learn anything? I want to hear from you!

## DIRECTIONS

Gather all of your friends and family who love mushrooms!

I was feeling lazy one afternoon after working all day and didn't want to have to worry about doing a lot of dishes after cooking. After taking an inventory of what I had in my kitchen, I came up with the idea for this dish and I was so pleased at how easy and delicious it was. I only had lentil pasta at my apartment that day, so I have used that each time I have made this recipe, but you can absolutely use whatever kind of pasta works best for you.

Get a large pot, and put all the ingredients in. Turn the heat to high and bring the mixture to a boil. Cover, and reduce the heat to low, and let the mixture simmer, stirring every couple of minutes. As it simmers, the ingredients will all cook and soften and absorb the broth, and you will know the meal is done when the broth is all absorbed, after about 20 minutes. Test a piece of the pasta to make sure it is cooked to your liking. If it feels too firm, add another half cup of broth and continue to let it simmer until the pasta is to your liking.

# ONE POT MUSHROOM STROGANOFF

## INGREDIENTS

**5** Cups of mushroom broth
**1** Pound of pasta of choice (penne or fusilli or rotini or farfalle is best)
**1** Pound of sliced mushrooms
**1** Tsp garlic powder
**1** Medium sweet onion, diced
**2** Tbsp nutritional yeast
**⅓** Cup tahini sauce
**1** Tsp salt (more to taste if wanted)
**½** Tsp pepper
**1** Tsp umami seasoning

**SERVING SIZE :** 7-8 PORTIONS

**TOTAL TIME**: 35 MINUTES

**COST**: LESS THAN $16

## NUTRITIONAL INFO
**Calories:** 254 • **Protein:** 10g • **Carbs:** 30g
**Fat:** 9g • **Fiber:** 6g • **Sugar:** 3g

This is a good one to use all five sense; smell and pay attention to how the aroma changes as the meal cooks. Look at it while you stir it, and keep in mind how the mushrooms and the pasta change as they cook and absorb the broth. Use a spatula to feel the texture and softness of the pasta, listen as it simmers and make sure that it is not boiling too fast and that the heat isn't up too high. Finally, use your taste to make sure you have enough seasoning and that everything is cooked how you like it.

When it's done, sit back, relax, and be so happy you only have one dish to do. Now go do something fun! **And I am so proud of you.**

# ONE POT ORZO

## WITH SUNDRIED TOMATOES, PARSLEY AND CUCUMBERS

### INGREDIENTS

**2** Cups of orzo
**4-5** Cups of vegetable broth
**1** Medium cucumber, chopped
**½** Cup of sundried tomatoes
Dried is healthier but in oil will be less dry. Both are good!
**1** Medium red onion, chopped
**¼** Cup chopped parsley
**1** Tsp salt
**½** Tsp pepper
**½** Tsp paprika
**1** Tsp garlic powder
**1** Red onion

**SERVING SIZE :** 5 PORTIONS

**TOTAL TIME**: 35 MINUTES

**COST**: LESS THAN $15

## DIRECTIONS

This is a fun way to make a one pot dish in the summertime because there is a fresh crispness and lightness to it.  I love the red onion, sundried tomato, olive combination and using orzo as the base such a cute and fun way to enjoy those flavors.

Put the orzo, broth, sundried tomatoes and onion in a large saucepan.  Bring the heat to high and allow it to boil.  Once the broth is bubbling, reduce the heat right away and cover.  Let the mixture simmer for another 17-20 minutes.  The heat needs to be really low but just high enough to keep a super slight simmer.  Stir and check on it every 3 minutes and stir from the bottom so that you avoid the orzo sticking to the pan.  You will know it's done when all of the broth has been absorbed by the rice and it is soft and fluffy.  If you feel that the Orzo hasn't cooked enough when all of the

## NUTRITIONAL INFO

**Calories:** 130 • **Protein:** 4.4g • **Carbs:** 23.6g
**Fat:** <1g • **Fiber:** 3g • **Sugar:** 5g

broth is gone, add another ½ cup of broth and continue to let it simmer, covered, for another 4 minutes, until you are satisfied with the texture and softness of the orzo.

Take the mixture and dump it into a large bowl, add the spices, parsley and cucumber and stir. This is another one that is so good warm but also good cold. It makes enough for 5 servings so you can have it for dinner with the fam or your friends or you can use it for meals throughout the week.  However it is you enjoy it, I hope it makes you smile and makes you full. **I am so proud of you!**

# ONE POT SALSA QUINOA

## INGREDIENTS

**1** Red bell pepper, diced
**1** Green pepper, diced,
**1** 12 Ounce can of baked beans
**1** 12 Ounce can of corn
**½** Yellow or sweet onion, diced
**¼** Cup of canned diced green chilis
**1** 12 Ounce can of diced tomatoes
**1** Tsp garlic powder
**1** Tsp salt
**½** Tsp paprika
**1** Cup of quinoa
**2** Cups + 1 tbsp of vegetable broth
**1** Cup of beefless ground beef

**SERVING SIZE :** 5 PORTIONS

**TOTAL TIME**: 40 MINUTES

**COST**: LESS THAN $16

## DIRECTIONS

Ready to make some delicious "salsa" with baked beans and quinoa all in one pot? Hell Yea! If you decide to add the beefless ground beef it will add a bit to the cost of the meal a bit but if you feel like splurging, it can be a nice addition. It is definitely not needed, however.

Put 1 tbsp of vegetable broth into the large pot and add the diced peppers and onions. Bring the heat to medium, and stir the peppers and onions in the broth, letting them cook for 4 minutes. If you are using the beefless beef, this is when you will add that as well.

When the peppers have softened and start to become translucent, add the canned corn, baked beans, diced tomatoes, chilis and the seasoning and stir so everything

### NUTRITIONAL INFO
**Calories:** 291 • **Protein:** 14g • **Carbs:** 47g
**Fat:** 4g • **Fiber:** 8g • **Sugar:** 14g

is well mixed. Quickly add in the quinoa and the rest of the vegetable broth as well. Raise the heat slightly, so that it is between medium and high, and allow the broth to begin to boil. Once it starts bubbling, reduce the heat to low and cover. It will take about 25 minutes for the quinoa to completely cook and for all of the broth to get absorbed, but I would check on it every couple of minutes and stir so that all of the flavor gets evenly distributed and everything cooks evenly.

The quinoa will expand a lot, and this can serve about 10 people. This is good warmed up or cold, and it is a really easy, cheap option to bring to a get together or a potluck at work, or it can serve as several meals for dinner and/or lunch, so it's really cost effective.  This is an exclusive recipe that is ONLY in this cookbook, so I hope you enjoy it.  As always, take notes and pay attention to what works.  If there is a spice or something you think would make this dish even better for you, try it out and add it. Let me know what you think!  I can't wait to hear from you!

# PEAS AND LENTILS

## INGREDIENTS

**2** Cups of peas (if frozen, thawed out)
**2** Cups of whole lentils
**5** Cups of vegetable broth, or 2 bullion cubes mixed with 5 cups of water
**1** Cup of coconut milk
**½** Cup of barbecue sauce
**1** Tbsp Italian seasoning
**½** Teaspoon of hot sauce (optional)
**1** Tsp garlic seasoning
**1** Tsp onion seasoning
**1** Tsp salt
**½** Tsp smoked paprika
**⅓** Cup of sundried tomatoes

**SERVING SIZE :** 8 PORTIONS

**TOTAL TIME**: 50 MINUTES

**COST**: LESS THAN $15

## DIRECTIONS

This is a simple, cheap and easy way to get lots and lots of protein in a tasty tasty way! It also only needs one pot, so if you have a small stove, small counter space, or are even working with a hot plate all you need is a pot! It will need to simmer for about 45-50 minutes to get the lentils completely cooked.

Take the pot and add all of the ingredients, but only add 4 cups of broth. You can also use your creativity when it comes to the seasoning. For me, salt, smoked paprika and garlic powder are staples to make any "simple" dish flavorful and help elevate it. If you have something you like a lot and I didn't include it in the ingredients, add it in! This is the best way to learn to cook; trying new combinations and being creative. You learn by listening to your

## NUTRITIONAL INFO
**Calories:** 94 • **Protein:** 7g • **Carbs:** 10g
**Fat:** 0g • **Fiber:** 5g • **Sugar:** 2g

pallet and following your instincts. If you feel nervous, just add a little bit at a time.

Turn the heat to high and stir everything in the pot so that the seasoning and sauces spread evenly. Allow the broth to come to a boil, and when it does, cover the pot and reduce the heat to low. Let the lentils simmer, checking and stirring everything 10 minutes or so. It will be done after 50 minutes, when the lentils are soft, and the vegetable broth has been totally absorbed.

It is really important that the heat is not too high! If it is, the broth will evaporate, and the lentils will not soften all the way. It is also important to check on the mixture and stir it from the bottom of the pan so that it doesn't stick. If the lentils don't look soft and you are concerned that the

liquid has been absorbed too quickly, slowly add the remaining cup of vegetable broth. I came up with this recipe when I was living in a very small kitchen that only had 2 working burners and I didn't have a lot of dishes. These were ingredients I had in my house, so I threw them together and I loved how it came out. I also learned the rhythm of how lentils need to be cooked, and I practiced a LOT and have used many different vegetable combinations and seasonings. I wanted to share this particular one with you because it is very affordable to make a big pot, and it can last for 5-6 meals. Most of the time when I make this dish or one similar to it, I will have it for lunch for the next week, so it is an AWESOME option for vegan meal prepping.

Don't be intimidated! You can totally do this. Be patient, take your time, taste as you go (Make sure it's cool enough, don't burn your tongue!), and take notes if you feel like that will help! Pay attention to what you like, or what you think could be better. I hope you love this recipe and I really would love nothing more than if you enjoy it but change one or two things and make it your own. Don't be afraid to be creative and remember, everyone deserves to eat healthy and delicious food, and everyone deserves the chance to cook! I am so proud of you already!

# POTATO AND CARROT LENTILS CURRY

## INGREDIENTS

**3** Large gold or russet potatoes, chopped into ½ inch pieces
**1** Tbsp curry
**1** Tsp turmeric
**3** Carrots, chopped into ½ in pieces
**1 ½** Cup of red lentils
**½** Cup diced tomatoes, fresh or canned
**1** Tsp salt
**½** Cup chopped onion
**½** Tsp pepper
**2** Cloves garlic, minced
**5** Cups of vegetable broth
**½** Tsp cinnamon (optional)
**⅔** Cup olive oil
**1** Cup of Coconut Milk
**1** Tbsp and 1 tsp tomato paste

**SERVING SIZE :** 5 PORTIONS

**TOTAL TIME**: 40 MINUTES

**COST**: LESS THAN $14

### NUTRITIONAL INFO
**Calories:** 275 • **Protein:** 11g • **Carbs:** 24g
**Fat:** 10g • **Fiber:** 12g • **Sugar:** 4g

## DIRECTIONS

This is one of my favorite meals of all time. It's not shiny or showy or fancy, but it's hearty and warm and filling and delicious. I also just can't ever get enough of lentils. I truly believe they are the most ethical food you can eat because it takes hardly any resources to grow them, they have so much nutritional value, are so filling, can be combined with so many other delicious foods, and they are so affordable. You also can make so many servings with one or two cups. They are just a wonderful vehicle for flavor and goodness, and I hope you like making them this way as well.

In a large pot, heat the olive oil at medium. Add the onions, garlic, carrots and potatoes and stir so everything is covered with olive oil. Stir and continue to cook for 4 minutes, until the onions begin to soften.

Add the rest of the ingredients and raise the heat to high. Bring the pot to a boil; then stir, reduce heat to low and cover and allow the mixture to simmer for 25 minutes. Check on it every 5 minutes or so to give it a stir. As always, it is really important to make sure that the heat isn't too high and you want to check, stir and pay attention to how the lentils look while you are

cooking them. Make sure you are keeping them from sticking to the bottom of the pot. After 25 minutes  if you feel the lentils are not fully cooked (they should be soft and enlarged from all of the broth-you can also take a small taste and try it when it has cooled a bit), add another ½ cup of vegetable broth, and continue the simmer until it is absorbed.

This is a good one to practice not only cooking lentils but also being creative, you can change the recipe a little bit each time you make it, or you can stick to exactly these instructions if you love it as is.  I hope you enjoy it and I'm so proud of you!

# ONE POT VEGAN PEANUT LO MEIN

## INGREDIENTS

¾ Cup of creamy peanut butter
**1** Pound of spaghetti or lo mien noodles
**1** Cup of chopped sugar peas
**1** Cup of chopped peppers either sweet or bell
**1** Tsp salt
**6** Cups of vegetable broth
**1** Cup of coconut milk
**½ - 1** Tsp garlic powder (to taste)
**1** Cup of shredded cabbage
**½** Tsp pepper
**½** Smoked paprika
**½ - 1** Cup of crushed peanuts
**1** Tbsp sesame oil

**SERVING SIZE :** 6 PORTIONS

**TOTAL TIME:** 30 MINUTES

**COST:** LESS THAN $20

## NUTRITIONAL INFO

**Calories:** 421 • **Protein:** 15g • **Carbs:** 46g
**Fat:** 18g • **Fiber:** 4g • **Sugar:** 4g

## DIRECTIONS

ONE POT! All the ingredients go right in the pot! So good and so easy. It might seem to be too good to be true, but it's not. This is an easy and quick way to do a take on peanut/sesame dish that might be served at a Thai restaurant. You can use rice or lo mien noodles, but I have made it with 99 cent spaghetti noodles, and it worked great.

Get out your trusted large pot, and put everything except the peanuts into it (they will be used as a topping when everything is cooked).

Turn the heat to high and let the broth come to a boil. Cover the pot and bring the heat to low. It will take about 20 minutes for the pasta to absorb the broth and peanut butter and for the vegetables to cook. I suggest checking on it every 4 minutes or so and make sure that nothing is sticking to the bottom of the pot (it will if the heat is too high). Stir it gently and make sure that the liquid is at a slight simmer so that everything is cooking but you really want to make sure that the heat isn't too high. I can't stress this enough. This is a wonderful meal and I don't want you to ruin it! When all of the broth is absorbed and the noodles are soft and cooked, it is ready! Top it with some crushed peanuts and get ready to earn some serious bragging points with anyone you share this meal.

When I created this meal, I was on my massive one pot kick. I quickly learned that there are so many ways to make things really delicious with correct measurements and just one pot. Rice, Quinoa, pasta, barley and couscous are all terrific options to experiment with. Try different measurements of broth, but I have found that it is typically 2 cups of broth to 1 cup of dried food. I think that you should pick something that sounds good to you and go for it and invent a one pot meal of your own in the next month, and I would love love LOVE to hear how it goes so please let me know.

As always, take notes, pay attention to what works and the tastes and flavors you enjoy. Take pictures, tell your friends and be so proud of yourself and know that I am totally proud of you too!

# ROASTED VEGETABLES

## INGREDIENTS

**2** Sliced & chopped sweet potatoes into half moon shapes
**2** Sliced & chopped russet potatoes into half moon shapes
**1** Gold potato chopped & sliced into half moon shapes
**3** Carrots, chopped into ½ inch pieces
**2** Cups of brussel sprouts
**1** White onion, chopped in half then cut the short way so they are long slivers
**1** Tbsp olive oil
**1** Tsp salt (more to taste)
**1** Tsp garlic powder
**½** Tsp pepper
**½** Tsp turmeric (optional)
**½** Tsp paprika (optional)

**SERVING SIZE :** 6 PORTIONS

**TOTAL TIME**: 1 HOUR

**COST**: LESS THAN $14

## NUTRITIONAL INFO
**Calories:** 114 • **Protein:** 4g • **Carbs:** 20g
**Fat:** 0g • **Fiber:** 4g • **Sugar:** 4g

## DIRECTIONS

Ahhhhh roasted vegetables. These have a special place in my heart. I am the oldest of 5 children and my mom was an outstanding and wonderful baker and had a few dishes she loved to cook, but she was very busy. She also was dealing with feeding 7 people and making sure everyone liked what was for dinner, so quite often, it was roasted vegetables. I used to think they were boring but now I could eat them every day. They are like a wonderful time machine back to the kitchen in the house I grew up in and no matter where I lived in the country, it was a little piece of home. They are also affordable and easy and there are many options of how to make them.

Preheat the oven to 425 degrees and grease a baking dish or cookie sheet. Arrange the vegetables and drizzle the olive oil on top and spread the seasoning over all of the of the vegetables. Toss them around to make sure everything is evenly mixed, and the seasoning and flavors are dispersed. Put them in the oven, and after 20 minutes, stir the vegetables to ensure that they all cook evenly, return to the oven and roast for another 25 minutes.

I like the metaphor of getting back to my roots with these root vegetables. They are so wholesome and not processed and delicious. These ingredients will make a lot of food, so enjoy this recipe for a whole week if you want to. **I hope you love it and I'm so proud of you!**

# TURMERIC LENTILS WITH VEGGIES

## INGREDIENTS

**2** Cup green lentils
**4** Cups vegetable broth
**4** Stalks of asparagus, chopped
**1** Medium zucchini, chopped
**1** Small red onion, chopped
**2** Cloves of garlic, minced
**1** Large red pepper, chopped
**2** Tsp turmeric
**2** Tsp salt
**½** Tsp pepper
**⅓** Cup olive oil

**SERVING SIZE :** 6-8 PORTIONS

**TOTAL TIME**: 50 MINUTES

**COST**: LESS THAN $15

## NUTRITIONAL INFO
**Calories:** 140 • **Protein:** 6g • **Carbs:** 13g
**Fat:** 6g • **Fiber:** 4g • **Sugar:** 3g

## DIRECTIONS

This is a slightly modified take on one of the recipes on my Blog, I have adjusted it so that it is a One Pot meal so it's nice and easy with minimal clean up!

Start by adding the olive oil and the vegetables to the pot, bring the heat to medium and coat the vegetables with the oil and cook for 4 minutes, allowing them to begin to soften.

Add all of the rest of the ingredients to the pot. Bring it to a boil, and then immediately cover and reduce heat to low. It should continue to simmer, and every 8-10 minutes or so, stir the lentils from the bottom of the pan to make sure they don't stick. After 40 minutes the lentils should be cooked through and softened. They should still be whole, rather than burst like in a lentil soup, but not firm. The vegetables will have softened and be a really nice compliment to the texture of the lentils.

This is another recipe I made with what I had on hand in the kitchen while living in a small space. It's a great chance to practice your lentil cooking, and the all of the spices in this one are so wonderful. You can use this for a whole week's worth of meals, and if you want to change it up, have it plain one day, in lettuce wraps another day, on a piece of avocado toast the next, and then come up with two of your own! As always, take notes if you feel like it will be helpful and add different seasonings that you like to make this dish personal for you.

# VEGAN CREAMY THAI ONE-POT PASTA

## INGREDIENTS

**1** Chopped sweet onion
**3** Minced cloves of garlic
**1** Pound of pasta
penne & fusilli are good suggestions
**1** Tsp curry powder
**¼** Cup tomato paste
**½** Tsp cumin
**½** Tsp turmeric
**½** Tsp graham masala
**1** Lime to juice
**2** Cups diced tomatoes
**1** Cup coconut milk
**2** Tablespoons of olive oil or coconut oil.
**1** Cup halved cherry tomatoes
**2** Tbsp chopped fresh parsley (optional)

**SERVING SIZE :** 6 PORTIONS

**TOTAL TIME**: 30 MINUTES

**COST**: LESS THAN $15

### NUTRITIONAL INFO
**Calories:** 149 • **Protein:** 5g • **Carbs:** 25g
**Fat:** 2g • **Fiber:** 4g • **Sugar:** 2g

## DIRECTIONS

This dish, like many in this book, was born from lack of space and only having 1 pot to work with.  I also didn't have a lid at that time, so I used a cookie sheet to cover it while it cooked.  There is nothing wrong with getting creative in order to make things work, so do what you have to do! This recipe is also a great example of how to use spices to create the flavors you need, and you can buy them for $1-$2 each and use them over and over again rather than spend $5 or $6 dollars or even more on a store bought sauce that probably won't even taste as good! So, get ready to make some flavorful magic.

In a large pot, heat the oil at medium heat.  Add the onion and garlic and turmeric, and stir about 3 minutes, until onions are translucent.

Add the rest of the ingredients except the cherry tomatoes to the pot, and raise heat to high, bringing the liquid to a boil.  When it reaches the boil, lower the heat to a med/low setting, and covered, allowing the food to simmer.  Stir every 4 minutes for about 18-20 minutes.  Make sure you are paying attention to the food, and that the pasta isn't sticking to the bottom.  As long as the heat is low enough and there is the right amount

of moisture, everything will be fine. Do a taste test if you want to be sure, but you will know it's done when there is no more excess moisture from the coconut milk and broth; finish by adding extra salt to taste, and garnish with parsley and halved cherry tomatoes.

I hope you feel great about this meal, please reach out to be with any questions or comments or to let me know how you personalized this recipe. I can't wait to hear and **I'm so proud of you!**

## DIRECTIONS

This dish is a nice way to enjoy lentils in the warmer months, as it has a less hearty taste and feels (to me at least) more summery thanks to the dill. Lentils with root vegetables became such a staple for me to make every Sunday and then eat throughout the week during the colder months, and I wanted a way to change it up and have something a bit lighter for the summer without having to break my routine because it was so easy and so cheap and so good. A lot of the time a meal that is associated with a particular season can be altered by one or two ingredients and it can transform the dish to be fitting and appealing for another time of the year.

To start, make sure everything is chopped and prepped, then add the onion, potatoes, carrots, 1 tsp salt and olive oil to a large pot. Heat over medium, stirring to coat the vegetables with the oil. Heat/stir for 6 minutes, allowing the vegetables to soften.

Add the lentils, coconut milk and 2 cups of vegetable broth to the pot. Bring the heat to high and stir so the lentils and vegetables are well mixed. Allow the liquid to come to a boil and add one more cup of the broth. Bring this to a boil, stir and cover, reducing the heat to med-low and allow the mixture to simmer. Every 3-4 minutes, uncover and stir from the bottom of the pot so ensure that the mixture

# VEGAN ONE-POT CREAMY LENTIL AND POTATO MASH
## WITH DILL

## INGREDIENTS

**4** Large russet or gold potatoes, chopped
**2** Cups of split lentils
**12** Ounces of coconut milk
**4** Large carrots, chopped
**4** Cups of vegetable broth
**1** Medium yellow onion, chopped
**3** Tbsp minced fresh dill
**2** Tsp salt
**½** Tsp pepper
**1** Tsp garlic powder
**1** Tsp paprika
**2** Tbsp of olive oil

**SERVING SIZE :** 6 PORTIONS

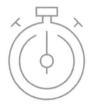

**TOTAL TIME**: 45 MINUTES

**COST**: LESS THAN $18

## NUTRITIONAL INFO
**Calories:** 337 • **Protein:** 14g • **Carbs:** 42g
**Fat:** 10g • **Fiber:** 8g • **Sugar:** 5g

doesn't stick. After 12 minutes, add the remaining cup of vegetable broth and the dill. Continue to let it simmer covered on med/low for 10 more minutes.

Because these are split lentils, rather than whole lentils, they form together while they are cooked and then blend with the potatoes and that is where the mashed potato texture comes from.

Remove from heat and stir; the texture should be similar to mashed potatoes. Serve warm, topped with extra dill.

**I would love for you to email me and let me know what you thought of this one; did you have any ideas you added to help make this dish summerier? I hope you love it and I'm so proud of you!**

# SOBA NOODLES WITH PORTABELLA MUSHROOMS & KALE

## INGREDIENTS

**½** Pound package of soba noodles, prepared as package directed or rice noodles or just regular old pasta
**2** Large portabella mushrooms, cut into **½** inch pieces
**2** Cups chopped kale leaves
**2** Cloves of garlic, minced
**1** Small red onion, diced
**⅓** Cup vegetable broth
**2** Tsp sesame oil
**1** Tsp salt

**SERVING SIZE :** 5 PORTIONS

**TOTAL TIME**: 25 MINUTES

**COST**: LESS THAN $20

## DIRECTIONS

For this one, you will need a large pot, as usual! The noodle package should have instructions on how to cook them, so follow along with those. Drain when they are done, and either store them in a bowl or in the strainer. Drizzle them with the sesame oil and give them a quick stir so that the noodles don't stick.

**Time for the vegetables!** In the same pot, add the vegetable broth, garlic and onion. Cook on medium/high heat for about 3 minutes, allowing the onions to soften. Add the portabella mushrooms and stir. The vegetable broth should reach a simmer. Continue to cook and stir until the mushrooms soften and begin to release moisture, around 5 minutes. Add the kale and salt, and continue to stir, allowing the greens to reduce in size, another 3 minutes.

### NUTRITIONAL INFO
**Calories:** 261 • **Protein:** 8g • **Carbs:** 22g
**Fat:** 15g • **Fiber:** 7g • **Sugar:** 5g

Remove the pan from the heat and transfer the noodles back into the pot with the vegetables; stir with the tongs so that all of the ingredients are evenly spread out.

I really like using vegetable broth because it is much healthier than olive oil, but it still has a lot of flavor. Pay attention to how the vegetables cook and notice any differences you see between how they cook in the broth versus roasting them or cooking them in oil.

This is a good one to eat as a group or to have as leftovers for a day or two. **I hope you love it and I'm so proud of you!**

# VEGAN SLOPPY JOES

## INGREDIENTS

**1** 12 Ounce can of corn
**2** Cups barbecue sauce
**1** Tbsp ketchup
**1** Tsp mustard
**1** Cup of cooked beets, chopped
**1** Tbsp worcester sauce
**2** Cups chopped red cabbage
**2** 12 Ounce cans of baked beans
**1** 12 Ounce can of black beans
**1** Small roma tomato, diced
**1** Small can green chilis
**2** Cloves garlic, minced
**1** Tsp salt
**1** Tsp smoked paprika

**SERVING SIZE :** 6 PORTIONS

**TOTAL TIME**: 15 MINUTES

**COST**: LESS THAN $15

## NUTRITIONAL INFO
**Calories:** 255 • **Protein:** 8g • **Carbs:** 48g
**Fat:** 1g • **Fiber:** 8g • **Sugar:** 28g

## DIRECTIONS

This is an easy, awesome way to enjoy the timeless classic that is the sloppy joe. This one is plant based but still just as sloppy, and I have worked it out for you so it's super affordable. Also, this is another recipe that makes 608 servings, but it might be hard to not eat it all yourself.

Get a large bowl and mix all of the ingredients. Stir well, allowing the sauces to spread and cover all of the ingredients. That's it! It's literally so easy! Serve on a bun or as a sandwich or on a portabella mushroom. **However it is that you eat it, enjoy!**

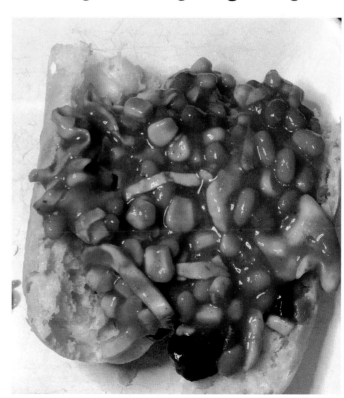

# ZUCCHINI, TEMPEH, BEET AND POTATO TACOS

## INGREDIENTS

¾ Cup of tempeh, chopped into small ½ inch pieces.
**1 ½** Tbsp taco seasoning
**1** Cup of vegetable broth
**1** Yellow onion, chopped
**½** Tsp pepper
**1** Tsp smoked paprika
**1** Tsp cumin
**2** Large potatoes, chopped into
**½** inch pieces
**1** Zucchini, chopped into small
**½** inch pieces
**⅓** Cup of olive oil
**1** Cup of chopped beets

**SERVING SIZE :** 4 PORTIONS

**TOTAL TIME**: 35 MINUTES

**COST**: LESS THAN $20

## NUTRITIONAL INFO
**Calories:** 142 • **Protein:** 9g • **Carbs:** 27g
**Fat:** 3g • **Fiber:** 4g • **Sugar:** 5g

## DIRECTIONS

Get ready for a fun, affordable and vegan take on tacos! Vegetables are great fillers and can work just as well, if not better, than any meat option.

**Here we go!**

If it is cheaper to buy raw beets than cooked ones, no problem! Just put them in a pot and cover with water, bring the pot to a boil and let it go for 45 minutes. You can prep everything else while they are cooking and even start working on sautéing the other vegetables.

Heat the olive oil in a large frying pan over med/high, and add the potatoes, zucchini and onion. Stir, and sautéed for 8 minutes, turning frequently, and allowing the vegetables to brown and become crispy.

Add the vegetable broth, tempeh and all of the seasonings to the pan, and stir. Bring to a simmer, and continue to move the mixture around, letting it cook for 10 minutes. Add the beets last and stir them in and cook for another 3 minutes.

Remove from heat and serve on taco shells topped with guac and/or salsa and/or vegan cheese. Taco Tuesday has never been better! It also works just on its own if you prefer and you can eat it for a couple days. **Amazing Job and I'm so proud of you!**

# VEGETABLE DRAWER NOODLES WITH JACKFRUIT & CHILI SAUCE

## INGREDIENTS

**1** Package of ramen noodles, cooked according to the instructions
**1** 20 Ounce can of jackfruit
**⅓** Cup siracha sauce
**1** Tsp chili flakes
**2** Cloves minced garlic
**1** Tsp salt
**1** Cup vegetable broth
**½-1** Cup of fresh chopped basil
The vegetables of your choosing (see suggestions), chopped
**1** Tbsp olive oil
**1** Tbsp tahini sauce

**SERVING SIZE :** 5 PORTIONS

**TOTAL TIME**: 35 MINUTES

**COST**: LESS THAN $20

## NUTRITIONAL INFO
**Calories:** 115 • **Protein:** 4g • **Carbs:** 14g
**Fat:** 2g • **Fiber:** 8g • **Sugar:** 2g

## DIRECTIONS

This is for my spicy people out there! I am a wimp with spice, but this one is exciting and a nice way to change it up from my normal routine, or a great meal to make for my friends who are a bit braver.

Pick the noodles that work best for you based on taste and cost and cook them according to the packaging. When they are done, toss them in a bowl with a little bit of olive oil to keep from sticking.

In a small bowl, whisk together the siracha and chili flakes. This is going to be spicy, so test it to make sure you like it and that it's not too intense. If you prefer less spicy, you can balance it out with tahini sauce. Set the sauce aside with the noodles.
Time to cook the vegetables! So, I named this "vegetable drawer ramen" because I

literally made this with the vegetables I had in my fridge. Zucchini and peppers work great, but whatever you chose to use, chop them up and place them into the same pot you cooked the noodles in and add the garlic, salt and vegetable broth. Sauté, stirring frequently so the vegetables can cook evenly, for about 7-8 minutes until they are soft. If you prefer more crunch, cook for less time and if you prefer softer, cook closer to 9 minutes. The broth should be totally cooked off.

Mix the vegetables with the noodles and chili sauce in a large bowl, toss in the basil, and serve warm or cold. Make sure you have a glass of water nearby to help with the spice!

**I would love to hear what vegetables you used for this and I am so proud of you!**

# MULTI BEAN SALAD

## INGREDIENTS

**1** 12 ounce can kidney beans
**1** 12 ounce can white beans
**1** 12 ounce can black beans
**1** 12 ounce can corn
**¾** Cup diced mango
**½** Cup chopped cilantro
(optional)
**½** Chopped red onion
**2** Large green peppers
(optional)
**1** Tsp salt
**1** Tsp paprika
**1** Tsp lime juice
**½** Cup olive oil

**SERVING SIZE :** 8 PORTIONS

**TOTAL TIME**: IF YOU
ROAST AND INCLUDE THE
PEPPERS: 1 HOUR
IF YOU DONT: 5 MINUTES

**COST**: LESS THAN $12

## NUTRITIONAL INFO
**Calories:** 115 • **Protein:** 4g • **Carbs:** 14g
**Fat:** 2g • **Fiber:** 8g • **Sugar:** 2g

## DIRECTIONS

Beans are freaking awesome. They are cheap and fill you up so much! Yay!

Adding the roasted peppers is optional. I think it elevates the dish a lot but if you don't have an oven or don't have time it still tastes really good with the beans. If you are adding the peppers: Preheat the oven to 450 and grease a baking pan. Slice the peppers in half, seed them and place them on the sheet, drizzle with olive oil and when the oven is heated, Roast for 15 minutes, removing from the oven before the peppers begin to get soft.

Allow them to cool, then dice them. Add them to a large bowl, and just mix the rest of the ingredients right in there. Top with lime juice.

This one is so simple it almost seems too good to be true, but it's not! It's really affordable and really delicious. You can use your creativity on this as well! If you prefer one type of beans, add those. If you want to try making the beans from scratch, check out the page on how to cook beans and go for it! Add any extra spices that you think taste good and test out some different flavors. These are your taste buds to satiate and your body to feed so do what makes you feel good! This is another meal you can use all week for your lunch and impress your coworkers with how bad ass and healthy you are. Also, A quick tip for those who are riding a bike to and from the

grocery store and using a backpack to carry your groceries:  Put the cans at the very bottom of the backpack, and also utilize the water bottle pockets or any other pockets on the side of your backpack if you have them.  It makes it way easier to get home!  I hope you enjoy this meal; You rock and I'm proud of you.

Devon has been passionate about cooking and recipe development since 2009. She is constantly creating new meals and configuring ways to make her vegan diet as exciting and delicious as possible, and nothing makes her happier than sharing her recipes with her readers and audience. She often says that cooking is her favorite creative outlet.

She graduated with her BA in English Literature from the University of Connecticut in 2010 and from George Washington University's Coding Bootcamp in 2019. She also spent a year volunteering with Americorps and is a certified yoga teacher. These experiences are some of what has helped shape her journey to where she is today: living as a happy and healthy sober vegan who wants to use her story to inspire others.

She runs and manages the popular vegan recipe blog "Getmetherecipe.com" and co-host the Get Me The Recipe Podcast with her brother, David. For fun she loves to listen to podcasts, watch Marvel Movies and the Real Housewives, and spend time with her family and friends. She also is the proud owner of the cutest dog in the world.

Learn more about Devon and her cooking adventures on her blog, or follow her on instagram at **@getmetherecipe.**

# ABOUT THE DESIGNER

Lauren is a graphic designer who graduated with a BFA from William Paterson University in 2016. She fell in love with design after taking a computer graphic's class in high school, and couldn't get enough. She would skip her lunch period eager to finish her projects and work on personal side projects, as well as just exploring the adobe programs to learn more about them. From there, she grew a passion for logo design, photo editing, branding, typography and layout design. Lauren happily considers design to be both her career as well as her hobby.

# ACKNOWLEDGEMENTS

Thank you to **Lauren Boggio** for your incomparable support and skills with designing the layout for this book. I could not have done this without you. Thank you to **Ali Andino** for helping out with some of the finishing touches. Thank you to **David Moran** for being the most supportive person imaginable. I don't know what I did to deserve you as a brother, but I am so happy you are mine. Thank you to **Rowen Moran, Rozzie Moran** and **Richard Moran** for your unwavering support and encouragement over the years and especially the last few months. Thank you to **Michael Moran** for teaching me the value of determination, integrity and hard work and for being so supportive of my passion and dream. Thank you to **Aimee Ouellette f**or believing in my when I didn't believe in myself, for telling me I wasn't crazy to try to write this book, and for being the best friend in the world. Thank you to **Alyssa Dolan** for being such a wonderful and supportive person in my life and for hyping me up everyday . Thank you to **Johnna Shura** for being in my life and being a constant rock of support that I don't want to even imagine my life without. Thank you to **Doc Cass f**or giving me the chance to cook for hundreds of people at the OBI Hostel many years ago. Thank you to **Dan Collins** for getting me interested in Vegan cooking. Thank you to any person who has read my blog, asked me for a recipe, or shown me any support over the years. And Finally, thank you to my mother, **Christan Moran**, who I feel with me in the kitchen every time I cook. I wish so much you were here with me, but I feel your pride and love with me every day.

GET ME THE RECIPE

vegan recipe blog

Made in the USA
Middletown, DE
14 January 2020